D0361615

1750

THE

WOLFF OLINS

GUIDE TO

CORPORATE

IDENTITY

Published in the United Kingdom in 1990 by

The Design Council

28 Haymarket

London SW1Y 4SU

Typeset, printed and bound in the United Kingdom by

Black Bear Press Limited

Cambridge

Designed by Wolff Olins/Hall

All rights reserved. No part of this publication may

be reproduced, stored in a retrieval system or transmitted

in any form or by any means now known or hereafter invented,

electronic, mechanical, photocopying, recording or otherwise,

without the prior written permission of the Design Council

© Wally Olins 1990

British Library Cataloguing in Publication Data

Olins, Wally

  The Wolff Olins guide to corporate identity. —Rev ed.

  1. Companies. Corporate identity

  I. Title

  659.285

  ISBN 0-85072-260-8

CONTENTS

Introduction

SECTION 1 — What it is 7

Products/services

Environments

Communications

Behaviour

The fundamental idea

SECTION 2 — Who it's aimed at 15

Internal and quasi-internal audiences

External audiences

SECTION 3 — Different identity structures 19

The monolithic identity

The endorsed identity

The branded identity

An identity for a subsidiary or a holding

SECTION 4 — Why and when to introduce it 29

Natural evolution

A catalyst for change

SECTION 5 — A corporate resource 33

Identity as a management resource

Role models — financial management and information technology
   management

SECTION 6 — How to introduce it **37**

Two levels

Consultants

How to pick a consultant

The place of advertising agents and PR companies

Working party

The stages of work

What will it all cost and how long will it take?

SECTION 7 — Research **53**

SECTION 8 — Risks **55**

SECTION 9 — Benefits **57**

Internal

Financial

Marketing

SECTION 10 — Examples **61**

Repsol

Prudential Corporation

Akzo

ICI

Conclusion **70**

Bibliography **73**

Appendix A — The basic elements **76**

Appendix B — Checklist of items **77**

Appendix C — Design advisory services **80**

INTRODUCTION

The first edition of the Wolff Olins Guide to Corporate Identity was published in 1984. It was an attempt to define and set boundaries around an activity which seemed to be emerging from cottage industry status.

Today, the corporate identity resource is becoming sophisticated and experienced. It is clear that corporate identity has begun to expand out of its graphic roots and embrace corporate communications, organisational behaviour and other non-design disciplines. However, the experience of the various practitioners in the field varies greatly, as does the way in which they define the subject.

Although corporate identity is now accepted as a mainstream management resource, things remain somewhat confused for the increasing numbers of organisations that seek to launch and maintain corporate identity programmes.

The brief for programmes may raise as many questions as it resolves:

- Does the proposed corporate identity relate both to the identity of the company and its brands?
- Should a company with an ancient and well-known but anachronistic name replace it with a new and unknown one?
- How can a company successfully present itself as coherent and single-minded to its shareholders and at the same time as a series of competing brands — or even totally different businesses — in the market place?
- Should a company replace or supplement all its acquisitions' names with its own name?

- Can a corporate identity help a company which is changing from commodity to high-technology, added-value businesses? If so, how?
- Can a clear corporate identity help a company to fight off an acquisition bid? If so, how?

Because corporate identity is both so simple and so profound it provokes controversy in the business world.

Are its proponents claiming too much for it? Is it simply a visual styling exercise — a kind of cosmetic? Is it merely a tool of marketing, or something rather bigger? Does it work?

All these and many similar questions are debated whenever corporate identity is seriously discussed.

This revised edition of the Wolff Olins Guide to Corporate Identity is concerned to give a brief, clear, state-of-the-art description of corporate identity for the benefit of those organisations who want to know what it is and find that they may have use for it.

Wally Olins
February 1990

SECTION 1

What it is

All organisations communicate all the time. Everything that they make or do or say — or don't say — is a form of communication. The totality of the way the organisation presents itself and is seen to be can be called its identity.

So all organisations have an identity whether they are aware of it or not. The process usually described as corporate identity consists of the explicit management of some or all of the ways in which the company's activities are perceived.

Corporate identity can project three things:

- Who you are
- What you do
- How you do it

Corporate identity manifests itself primarily in three major areas which you can see:

- Products and services — what you make or sell
- Environments — where you make or sell it
- Communications — how you explain what you do

  And one which is not visible:

- Behaviour

PRODUCTS / SERVICES

Sometimes the product and how it performs is much the most significant factor in influencing how the organisation as a whole is perceived. It is, for example, the appearance and performance of a Jaguar car which largely influences the way we perceive the identity of the company that makes it.

In a product based organisation, the product itself,
what it costs, how it performs and what it looks like
influences what we think of the company.
Above – Bang & Olufsen hi-fi system.

ENVIRONMENTS

In some organisations, like retail stores, hotels and leisure centres, the environment is crucial in presenting the idea that the organisation represents to its customers (eg Claridge's).

In any event, all organisations have offices, canteens, factories or other places in which they live and carry out their work, and these exercise a powerful influence on the way both employees and outsiders see the organisation.

COMMUNICATIONS

Every company communicates, both to its own staff and to a variety of outside audiences. The communication process embraces all the printed material that the organisation uses, from invoices through to press advertising, together with communication in other media, TV, events, new-product launches and so on. The totality of the communication process influences the way in which different audiences perceive the organisation.

There are some companies whose products and brands largely derive their identity from the packaging, advertising and other promotional material with which they are surrounded. In this case communication almost entirely conveys the identity idea (eg Persil).

BEHAVIOUR

There are some organisations whose personality and style emerge not so much through what they look like, what they make or where they live, as through the way in which they behave.

Top – Public spaces at Claridge's Hotel, London. The name and reputation evokes the idea of understated luxury which derives directly from Claridge's physical environment.

Bottom – Communication through advertising has made Persil so powerful a brand, that most consumers neither know nor care who makes it. In fact the brand name is shared between Unilever who market Persil in Britain and France (right) and rivals Henkel who use it everywhere else (left).

These are, for the most part, service organisations like banks, airlines, police forces, health authorities, and so on. A common characteristic of such organisations is that it is the most junior staff who have the most contact with the outside world and are therefore largely responsible for establishing how the organisation as a whole is perceived.

THE FUNDAMENTAL IDEA

The fundamental idea behind a corporate identity programme is that in everything the company does, everything it owns, and everything it produces, the company should project a clear idea of what it is and what its aims are. The most significant way in which this can be done is by making everything in and around the company — its products, buildings and communications — consistent in purpose and performance and, where this is appropriate, in appearance too.

Inevitably then, the visual elements that go to make up the corporate identity usually make the most significant impact. Linked to these is the way in which the company behaves and the language it uses.

Outward consistency of this kind will only be achieved, and for that matter is only appropriate, if it is the manifestation of an inward consistency — a consistency of purpose within the organisation. However, consistency must not be confused with uniformity.

It can be desirable, depending on the corporate objectives, to identify parts of the corporation independently. But even variety of this kind must be handled consistently (see Section 3).

The elements that go to make up the visual system are outlined in Appendix A.

The items over which a visual identity is normally applied are listed in Appendix B.

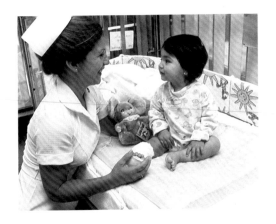

In service organisations, airlines, police forces, hospitals, restaurants and so on it is usually the most junior staff who have the greatest influence on the way the organisation is perceived, because of the way in which they behave to the public.

SECTION 2

Who it's aimed at

The audiences of an organisation are those people who come into contact with it at any time, in any place, and in any form of relationship.

It is often assumed that the most important audience for any company is its customers but there are, of course, many groups of people working in and around an organisation who will have contact with it. These are some:

INTERNAL AND QUASI-INTERNAL AUDIENCES

- All staff, at all levels, in all companies and divisions, in all countries
- Representatives of trade unions
- Shareholders
- Directors
- Pensioners
- Families of employees

EXTERNAL AUDIENCES

These are some of the main external audiences:

- Central government, local government, MPs and local councillors
- Competitors
- Suppliers
- Customers, both direct and indirect
- Opinion formers
- Journalists
- Investment analysts, merchant bankers, stockbrokers
- Potential recruits
- Schools and universities
- Trade and industry associations

These audiences are not always separate and independent. To some extent they are overlapping. Pensioners, shareholders and journalists may also be customers. Customers may also be shareholders — or may want to be — and so on.

Different audiences will form a view of an organisation based on the totality of the impressions that the company makes on them. Where these impressions are contradictory — where impressions made in one place are different from those made somewhere else — the overall impression will be negative, or at any rate confusing.

SECTION 3

Different identity structures

The identities of most companies which have given consideration to the matter fall, more or less, into one or other of three categories. These categories are not mutually exclusive and rigidly defined. There is some overlap. But for the most part they serve as a useful guide.

Each of these categories has advantages and disadvantages. None is intrinsically superior to any of the others. Each is appropriate in different commercial circumstances. When circumstances change it is sometimes appropriate to change or modify structures.

Monolithic

This is where the organisation uses one name and one visual system throughout (eg Mitsubishi, IBM, Sony, BP).

Endorsed

This is where the companies forming a group are perceived either by visual or written endorsement to be part of that group (eg General Motors — Vauxhall, Opel, Buick, Cadillac, Chevrolet etc; United Technologies; Trafalgar House).

Branded

This is where the company operates through a series of brands or companies which are apparently unrelated, both to one another and to the corporation (eg General Foods, Unilever, Procter & Gamble).

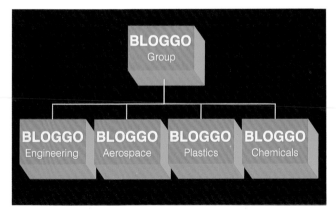

Monolithic

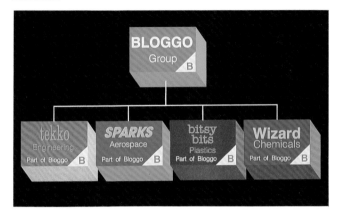

Endorsed

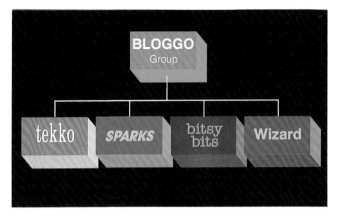

Branded

THE MONOLITHIC IDENTITY

Companies operating a monolithic identity normally have the following characteristics.

- They have grown largely organically (eg IBM, Porsche, Sony).
- They operate in a relatively narrow band of activities which the consumer sees as being closely related to each other — retailing, the oil industry, airlines.
- They tend to be proud of their products, their staff and their customer relations.
- They often operate at the upper end of the market.

However, there are a number of companies using the monolithic system, primarily Japanese, which have very broad product ranges (eg Mitsubishi — cars, foods, banking, equipment; Yamaha — equipment, musical instruments and motorcycles). These companies traditionally believe that the corporation's reputation can be extended to cover a broad range of products.

- The fundamental strength of the monolithic identity is that because each product and service launched by the organisation has the same name, style and character as all the others, everything within the organisation by way of promotion or product supports everything else. Relations with staff, suppliers and the outside world are clear, consistent, relatively easy to control and usually cheaper and more economical.
- Companies with monolithic identities tend, as a consequence, to have high visibility, which can be a great advantage in the market place.

Some Japanese companies use a single name over a wide variety of activities. Mitsubishi (above) use their name for cars, consumer goods, aircraft, food, banking – and other activities.

THE ENDORSED IDENTITY

Since a large number of companies have grown largely by acquisition and seek to employ the endorsed identity system, this is perhaps the most significant category, at least in numbers. United Technologies, General Motors, Trafalgar House and P&O all employ variations of an endorsed identity system.

Companies which project an endorsed identity normally have the following characteristics.

- They have grown largely by acquisition. Often they have acquired competitors, suppliers and customers, each with its own name, culture, tradition and reputation amongst its own network of audiences.

- They are multi-sector businesses, operating in a wide band of activities — manufacturing, wholesaling, retailing, selling components to competitors, making finished products themselves and so on.

- They are concerned to retain the goodwill associated with the brands and companies which they have acquired, but at the same time they want to superimpose their own management style, reward systems, attitudes and sometimes name upon their subsidiaries.

- They have certain audiences, such as financial audiences, opinion formers, possibly some suppliers and customers and so on, whom they want to impress with their total size and strength. Among these groups, they will want to emphasise uniformity and consistency as opposed to diversity.

- Often they have acquired competitive ranges of products. They therefore have problems of competition, even confusion, among suppliers, customers and often their own employees.

- They frequently operate in many different countries in which their products and their reputations vary.

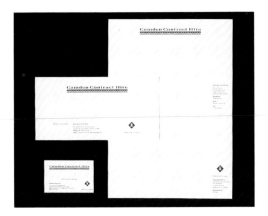

Mercantile, an interesting and complex example of endorsed identity, created by Wolff Olins. The Mercantile group embraces a wide range of different activities; including leasing of various kinds, car rental and vehicle distribution. All its activities are endorsed by the Mercantile mark (middle). Mercantile itself is part of the Barclays banking organisation.

Companies seeking to create a corporate identity covering a wide range of activities, with subsidiaries that have differing and frequently competitive backgrounds, face a complicated task. On the one hand, certainly at the corporate level and for corporate audiences, they want to create the clear idea of a single, but multi-faceted organisation that has a sense of purpose. On the other, they want to allow the identities of the numerous companies and brands they have acquired to continue to flourish in order to retain goodwill, both in the market place and among employees.

This requires a very difficult balancing act. These aims cannot, without the greatest possible sensitivity, be achieved simultaneously.

THE BRANDED IDENTITY

Some companies, for the most part those in pharmaceuticals, food, drink and other fast-moving consumer goods, sometimes separate their identities as corporations from those of the brands which they make and sell (eg Procter & Gamble, Unilever and BSN). At the corporate level, these companies reach out to all of the audiences of the monolithic or endorsed company, but they do not present their corporate face to the consumer. So far as the final customer is concerned, the corporation does not exist. What the customer perceives is only the brand. The reasons some companies pursue this policy are that:

- The long-standing tradition of the fast-moving consumer goods industry is that the consumer is readily influenced by basic and obvious symbolism (eg Sunlight = clean, Brut = macho, Alpen = wholesome). This somewhat naive symbolism seems inappropriate for a sophisticated and complex corporation.

Crown is a major paint brand. Although corporate ownership has changed over the years, and the brand has evolved organically and through acquisition, the brand values and identity remains strong and consistent. Above – packaging and vehicle liveries by Wolff Olins.

- Brands may have a cycle or life of their own, quite distinct from that of the company.
- Brands from the same company may well compete in the market place and their integrity might appear to be damaged in the eyes of the consumer if they were known to come from the same stable.
- Brands should be free to develop powerful identities of their own, appropriate to their consumers.

AN IDENTITY FOR A SUBSIDIARY OR A HOLDING

Throughout this section, and indeed elsewhere in this guide, it has been assumed that identity should embrace the totality of the organisation. While this is often the case, it frequently happens that divisions or semi-autonomous subsidiaries of corporations may feel the need for separate identity programmes. Sometimes the reverse situation operates and the holding wishes, for sound commercial reasons, to separate itself from one or all of its subsidiaries (eg Kingfisher). This situation occurs particularly among companies with endorsed or branded identities.

There is no reason why such programmes should not be undertaken, but it is important to take into account the attitudes, style and opinions of the corporate whole.

It is usually best to clarify relationships with the corporate holding company before embarking on the programme.

SECTION 4

Why and when to introduce it

NATURAL EVOLUTION

Most companies grow up with an identity which has emerged naturally as part of what they are. The identity has often been developed intuitively, in a fragmented, even muddled fashion. Often the identity is a manifestation of the personality of the founder — it bears his or her name and imprint.

Then there comes a moment when this somewhat casual, organic and uncultivated identity gets out of step with reality.

Here are a few examples of how this might happen:

- The company finds that it has a number of major activities, some of which are rapidly growing, but its name and reputation remain associated with its original business, a small and perhaps declining proportion of the whole.

- The company acquires or merges with a major corporation whose activities only slightly overlap with its own. It needs to create a single new organisation embracing the traditions and loyalties of the original companies, in order to allow the new company to emerge.

- The company changes its direction and moves, say, from commodity to higher-added-value, high-technology products, but its reputation is out of step with the reality.

- The company finds its smaller brands are being squeezed out of the market. It needs to use the strength of its corporate name to add weight to its brands.

- The company grew organically and by opportunistic acquisition. It is known in the market place for some of its more glamorous but less profitable businesses. There is dissatisfaction internally and externally because its real strengths go unnoticed.

- The company is concerned that it is vulnerable to predators who may seek to acquire it, at a time when its real size and strength are not generally appreciated.
- The organisation seeks to make acquisitions. It therefore needs to present itself as an attractive and comprehensible proposition to takeover candidates.
- The company needs to create better and more effective co-ordination between its different divisions which are increasingly selling to the same customers, and buying from the same suppliers.
- The organisation duplicates its research and development efforts and misses opportunities to develop new products because there is insufficient internal co-operation.

So a new corporate identity is normally introduced at a time of merger, diversification, reorganisation, or other strategic structural and management change. Its purpose is very often to underline the new sense of direction internally, manifest it externally, and act as a catalyst so that change can continue with minimum dislocation and maximum acceptance.

A CATALYST FOR CHANGE

Corporate identity is often a massive catalyst for change. This is because if a corporate identity programme is to work effectively, it will be concerned with three areas of corporate activity each of which is fundamental to the nature and purposes of the organisation. The three areas are; coherence, personality and positioning.

Coherence

An intention of all corporate identity programmes is to create visual coherence. Visual coherence cannot be superimposed on an inchoate structure. In order to obtain visual coherence there must be structural coherence which in turn derives from strategic coherence. It follows then that a corporate identity programme must take into account both the strategy and structure of the organisation.

Personality

A powerful visual identity enables the organisation to symbolise its ethos, spirit and attitudes, so that everyone who works for it can share and then present the same standards to all the people who deal with it. It is not possible to symbolise an organisation visually and effectively without uncovering its culture, characteristics and personality.

Positioning

A corporate identity programme is intended to help an organisation to differentiate itself and its products from those of its competitors in the market place. This inevitably involves the consideration of product-related and marketing-related issues. A corporate identity programme therefore inevitably involves marketing issues.

If these three factors — coherence, personality and positioning — are taken into account, a properly conducted corporate identity programme becomes one of the means by which the organisation analyses its strengths and its weaknesses and subsequently positions itself.

That is why Wolff Olins sometimes describes corporate identity as corporate strategy made visible.

SECTION 5

A corporate resource

Changing a corporate identity is a profound step. It is one of the moments in an organisation's life when it stands back and looks at what it is, how it became what it is and what it is going to do and say about itself. Some companies initially feel an emotional antipathy to the conscious cultivation of identity. They feel that it is too self-conscious, even too manipulative.

However, the development and introduction of a new corporate identity brings with it the clear implication that the corporate reputation will no longer look after itself — it must be guarded as a corporate resource, in the same way that the corporation guards its research and development, investment, personnel and other corporate resources.

IDENTITY AS A MANAGEMENT RESOURCE

This does not happen without planning, sometimes accompanied by structural change. The process by which an identity is deliberately introduced or changed and consciously cultivated has to be thought through carefully. It sometimes means that organisational changes have to be made so that the job can be done in the most cost-effective fashion.

Identity should be regarded by management as a corporate resource and treated like any other significant corporate resource, like finance, investment, personnel, research and development, marketing, information technology and so on. Identity needs an appropriate power base, adequate funding and commitment. If it is given this backing it will operate just as effectively and give much the same value as any other corporate resource.

ROLE MODELS — FINANCIAL MANAGEMENT AND INFORMATION TECHNOLOGY MANAGEMENT

Perhaps the two most significant role models for identity management within the corporation are financial management and information technology management, both of which are accepted as entirely standard corporate resources in every major corporation. Financial management is significant because it is ubiquitous, traditional and very powerful. Information technology management is an important role model, because it is relatively new and it had to fight for recognition. When an organisation is looking for a way to treat its identity resources, it can help to use these as models upon which it should build up its identity management system.

SECTION 6

How to introduce it

The identity resource must be managed in broadly the same way as other resources within the organisation.

The following is an indication of the way in which identity is introduced and managed in most corporations. It should of course be regarded as a general rule rather than specific guide.

TWO LEVELS

- A corporate identity programme is managed at two levels — the top and the middle levels of the organisation. Without board commitment, and specifically chief executive commitment, it will not get off the ground and cannot be sustained. Without tight middle management control it will get bogged down and dribble away under the assaults of other middle managers who may see it as a threat to their authority.

- It is essential that the top is, and is seen to be, committed and that middle management control is introduced and then sustained.

- When a corporate identity programme has been decided upon, an executive working with the chairman or managing director must be given the task of managing the programme. Such a person will often, although not always, have a communication or marketing background.

CONSULTANTS

Organisations are rarely sufficiently objective, self-aware or experienced in the appropriate disciplines to carry out a corporate identity programme without external assistance.

A corporate identity programme should be carried out with the help of professional design consultants with a proven background in identity work.

HOW TO PICK A CONSULTANT

Normally corporate identity is regarded as the province of design consultants, some of whom specialise in this work.

Consultants should be appointed on the basis of their track record, their personality, their presentations, their proposed working methods and, of course, on whether the personal chemistry between them and the client is right.

Design consultants, however, vary a good deal. Some concentrate on the design rather than the analytical processes which precede them. Some have a characteristic visual style. A few have built up their businesses around identity work or are specialists in this field, others offer a wide range of design services. Some are familiar with large multinational companies and others are not. Their size varies from those with 300 staff to one-man bands. The range of choice is wide, so is the range of fees.

In the UK the Chartered Society of Designers (CSD), the Incorporated Society of British Advertisers (ISBA), the Design Council and similar bodies can provide a list of design consultancies. (See Appendix C for their addresses). In other countries similar trade bodies should be consulted. Advertising agencies and PR consultancies and other professional advisers can also be consulted for names where appropriate. The best recommendation, however, comes from those who have already used the consultancy service.

THE PLACE OF ADVERTISING AGENCIES AND PR COMPANIES

Developing a corporate identity is a specialised business. Although advertising agencies and PR companies can make a contribution at appropriate stages in the process, they are not, and for the most part do not purport to be, equipped to be main contractors in this kind of work.

Their value, both as advisers and practitioners, emerges when the corporate identity programme has been launched. At that point there is often a need for corporate advertising and internal/external communication work to complement and reinforce the identity effort.

WORKING PARTY

When a consultancy company has been appointed, a small working party or steering group should be formed of individuals from the consultancy and client organisation whose job it is to discuss the programme and work together on it — all the way through.

THE STAGES OF WORK

Although the process can be divided and sub-divided in a number of ways, the work can be conveniently broken down into the following stages:

- Stage 1

    Investigation, analysis and strategic recommendations.
- Stage 2

    Developing the visual identity.
- Stage 3

    Launch and introduction.
- Stage 4

    Implementation.

Stage 1 — Investigation, analysis and strategic recommendations

This stage consists of a research programme and a series of audits all conducted to find out how the organisation is perceived and why, leading to recommendations. The research embraces individuals representing different points of view both inside and outside the organisation.

The research involves interviews which are intended to find out how the organisation is perceived both internally and externally by the people with whom it comes into contact. The interview programme will normally be carried out by the corporate identity consultants. There are situations, however, in which it can be contracted out to a research company.

The number of interviews will vary according to the size and complexity of the organisation, from a minimum of 20–30 up to 200–300. In addition the consultancy will examine desk research produced by and for the organisation.

Every corporate identity programme will incorporate a design audit. The primary purpose of this is to examine the way in which the different parts of the organisation present themselves in terms of products, graphics and environments.

In certain programmes it may also be useful to undertake other kinds of audit. Increasingly corporate identity programmes involve audits of communications and behaviour as well as design. The communication audit examines how different parts of the organisation talk and listen and to whom. The behavioural audit is concerned with finding out what the different parts of the organisation are actually like to deal with. These audits may be undertaken by an appropriately equipped corporate identity consultancy or contracted out to a specialist.

The three audits, together with the desk research and the interview programme, are mutually reinforcing.

When all audits and research have been carried out the working party meets to consider the findings. After discussion the findings and recommendations on the existing identity and proposals for future work are formally presented to the board.

Findings and recommendations

The findings will focus on how the organisation is perceived and why.

Sometimes the conclusions will relate solely to issues concerned with visual identity. More often, though, the consultant's presentation will take account of the company's position in the market place, its strategy, its structure, its product range, its branding policies, its morale, and its geographical and functional organisation. The findings should take into account, above all, the ambitions of the company.

The findings will inevitably involve specific recommendations on the following:

- Whether to keep all existing names, to get rid of some, to modify others, to stick to one or whatever. In other words, it may recommend a monolithic, endorsed or branded identity.

- Whether to strengthen the existing visual identity (eg London Transport), to develop a modified identity derived from the existing identity (eg Pilkington, Renault), or whether to create an entirely new visual identity or identities appropriate to the culture, style and purpose of the corporation and (sometimes) its divisions and its brands.

The recommendations may also deal with other issues such as internal and external communication, behaviour and so on.

All of this leads to the development of the design brief.

Stage 2 — Developing the visual identity

Once the design brief has been agreed, the design consultancy starts to work out the design idea.

At the heart of the programme is the symbol or logotype, the colours and typefaces. The symbol is highly visible; its prime purpose is to present the idea of the corporation with impact, brevity and immediacy. It therefore encapsulates the entire identity idea. Because of this, it often becomes the focal point from which the whole identity is subsequently judged.

It is not always desirable to change the symbol. In some cases modification may be more appropriate. Organisations who have spent millions on promoting their symbols over years are more likely to wish to modify what they have than change it completely.

Equally, however, there are situations when it is desirable to make a clean break and produce a new visual solution. Usually this is because the existing visual style no longer presents the reality clearly. In this situation it is sometimes the case that names are also changed.

Every case must be examined on its merits. The decision to change a name and symbol must not be taken lightly, nor should it be baulked simply because of potential difficulties.

Some of the issues that will affect the decision are:

- The nature of the business that the company is in.
- Its reputation within the business.
- Its plans for growth and development.
- The extent to which perceptions of the organisation are in line with the realities.

The consultancy will normally produce a series of optional design approaches which it will show in sketch form across an appropriate range of activities. These approaches should, whenever possible, represent different ways of dealing with the problem. Each of these approaches will be monitored and discussed by the working party to see how closely each fits with the design brief. Eventually one approach will be chosen and developed.

The chosen design scheme is then worked up for a presentation showing how the various applications will work on buildings, advertisements, literature, vehicles, uniforms and so on.

The approved sketches must be developed into artwork and then fine tuned so that they are usable across a wide range of materials (eg plastics, paper, metal) and a wide range of sizes (eg buttonhole badges, neon signs) in a wide range of countries with differing technical facilities, by people inside and outside the company with varying skills, knowledge and interest.

The process works in the following way:

- First, basic elements are produced from artwork (see Appendix A).
- Second, from these basic elements a wide range of typical applications for use is prepared, covering, say, stationery, signs and shop interiors (see Appendix B).

Repsol derives from INH the Spanish state owned oil company.

Top – some of the names and logotypes used within INH.

Bottom – a 1989 Repsol service station incorporating the new identity programme created by Wolff Olins.

- Third, both the basic elements of the artwork and some of the applications start to be codified in the form of a design manual or guide. This document eventually contains examples of all major applications of the corporate identity programme and should be widely distributed and used both by the company and its appropriate suppliers. Although preparation of the document starts during Stage 2, it usually emerges during Stages 3 and 4.

Stage 3 — Launch and introduction

If the new corporate identity programme is to be implemented successfully it has to be launched with enthusiasm and commitment.

At the launch of a new identity programme management has an opportunity to explain what the organisation is, where it has come from, where it thinks it is going and how the new identity will help it get there.

It is essential that identity is seeded into the organisation and managed as a corporate resource in exactly the same way as other corporate resources.

The launch of an identity programme takes place in two phases. People inside the company must be committed to the new identity before it emerges, so it is essential that the internal launch of an identity programme takes place before the external launch.

The internal launch normally takes the form of seminars, discussions and audiovisual presentations; while the external launch involves advertising, brochures, sales meetings and often a quite complex press relations drive.

It is sometimes appropriate to use sophisticated audiovisual techniques at major events.

Naturally where the company has a dealer organisation the external launch should be divided into two stages — dealer and special customer launch, followed by a public launch.

Stage 4 — Implementation

Cost and time schedules

A cost, time and method schedule for the launch and subsequent implementation of the programme must be prepared at the same time as detailed design work is taking place.

The following factors have to be taken into account:

- Who will be responsible for running the programme inside the company? It is essential that this job is held by an executive with influence, tact and preferably experience. He or she will be responsible directly to the chief executive and may be called Design Manager, Communications Manager, or Identity Manager.

- At what speed is the implementation programme going to be managed? There are four choices here:

    — An overnight change from old to new.
    — A controlled change taking place very quickly, say over a period of a year.
    — A controlled but more gradual change, say over 3–5 years.
    — Gradual replacement on an ad hoc basis.

The method chosen depends upon how dramatic the identity change is — the more dramatic the change, the more rapidly the new identity should be introduced — what the economic climate is, what the marketing and internal issues are and so on.

Methods of control

In addition, the corporate identity resource has to be established with a clear brief, adequate funding and appropriate lines of authority. Here are some of the issues that have to be resolved:

- Who is going to pay for the programme — the centre or the operating units?
- How should liaison between different companies and geographic divisions and the central identity resource work?
- How should the resource be manned and how many staff should it have?
- Where should it be located?
- What are the lines of responsibility?

Implementation

There is always a danger that after the excitement of the investigation, design and launch work the implementation of the identity programme will be neglected.

That is why implementation is the most important stage. If after all the preparatory work nothing really happens, everything that has gone before is wasted.

Implementation is essentially a long-term process. It is to do with getting people inside the organisation to develop a clear instinct, intuition or feel for what is and what is not appropriate for the organisation.

At one level it is to do with substance — stationery, signs, packaging, replacing one set of colours and one logotype with another — and here the control manual (preparation of which begins in Stage 2) is a vital tool.

At a more basic and significant level, however, it is to do with emotion — creating a situation in which people both inside and outside the company develop a feeling for what is appropriate. The identity programme cannot rely altogether upon the manual. The management of the organisation must create and sustain a sense of commitment.

Implementation of a corporate identity must never stop. It must always battle against the apparently easier way.

As the company changes, acquires new subsidiaries, moves into new activities and develops new products, the corporate identity must be used appropriately and modified when necessary. The identity must adapt to new situations as they develop.

Implementation is managed by the Identity Manager who is sometimes responsible for other related activities — internal communications, PR and so on. He or she is normally responsible for the implementation of the programme to the chief executive and the working party.

The board must be seen to be consistently committed to the programme.

The corporate identity programme will have an impact on brands, branding and product design, on the design and maintenance of buildings, on advertising campaigns, and on a wide variety of other corporate activities.

Essentially, running an implementation programme effectively depends on achieving the appropriate balance between the requirements of different departments and divisions with differing priorities and the requirements of the corporation as a whole.

From time to time there will be a conflict of interest or opinion between the functional divisions and departments and the Identity Manager. Where the dispute cannot be resolved at an appropriate level, it should go for arbitration. The working party, or another appropriate body, should meet regularly, say every two months, to review progress on the identity and to arbitrate where necessary between the differing interests within the organisation.

WHAT WILL IT ALL COST AND HOW LONG WILL IT TAKE?

A corporate identity programme is normally excellent value for money. For the price of a single campaign on television or in colour supplements it allows the company to make consistent, meaningful, co-ordinated and permanent impact throughout all its activities.

The cost depends largely upon timing. When an organisation is relaunching itself with a new name and visual identity it has to make a major impact, so it will have to move fast and the costs will be higher.

When, as is often the case, the existing identity is modified, the introduction can be lower key, the programme of implementation more gradual, and therefore the costs can be lower and spread out over a longer period.

Corporate identity costs are, apart from the origination work, usually dealt with as part of annual departmental budgets. Signs already get repainted, stationery gets reprinted, vehicles get replaced.

Costs can be divided up and examined in the following way:

- Consultant fees.
- Cost for creating new material (eg signs on buildings).
- Cost for launching the identity (eg advertising, videos etc).
- Replacement costs — those costs involved in replacing existing material which would have needed replacing anyway (eg stationery, vehicle liveries etc).

Each programme should be costed in stages. A fixed budget for time and fees should be established for Stages 1 and 2. Variations should be allowed for if the brief changes. There should be a clear separation between fees and outside costs.

Fees for Stages 3 and 4 should be negotiated as the project develops and its total approximate size can be estimated.

During the course of Stage 3, and more particularly during implementation (Stage 4), fees can be negotiated for separate projects.

SECTION 7

Research

Is it practical to research the proposed corporate identity before it is launched to see if it will work?

There are differing views on this. One respectable view is that it is possible to research individual parts of the proposed identity programme, such as the design elements — names, colours, symbols — and even the whole before it is launched. The argument goes that such research, while it will not certainly tell you what will work, will definitely tell you what won't.

Another view is that such research only succeeds in screening out the unorthodox and is therefore likely to be inhibiting rather than helpful.

As research techniques improve, it is clear that the risk-reduction process which research offers is becoming increasingly worthwhile.

In any event some research is vital. It is essential to go through all the proper procedures to check that any new names which may be proposed are both available and culturally and linguistically acceptable in all appropriate territories. It is also essential to check that designs do not infringe copyright and that they are culturally acceptable wherever the organisation operates.

After a programme has been launched, many companies carry out tracking studies to check the extent to which the new corporate identity programme has affected the awareness of different groups of people towards the organisation. Such studies are almost always worthwhile.

SECTION 8

Risks

Do corporate identity programmes ever go wrong? Do they destroy existing identities and replace them with new ones which are inappropriate and therefore bring the company and its products into disrepute?

Like any business decision involving change, there is sometimes some risk in changing identity. Usually, however, identity change is linked with a series of other changes which modify the character of the organisation, and the identity change is one of the means by which other change can be dramatically presented. In this context, therefore, to talk of risk is to miss the point.

However, a change in identity can bring direct commercial risk where packaging is changed, shops are re-designed or some other direct and clear marketing change is made. In these cases the normal commercial risk-reduction procedures involving research must be undertaken.

When an identity programme misfires, however, it is normally not because there is something wrong with the name or because the design work is found to be unacceptable culturally, but because it does not receive adequate management support and resources. If the new identity is not enthusiastically and continuously supported from the beginning it may be rejected by the divisions (perhaps concerned about losing a degree of independence) and it may therefore collapse or simply wither away. Properly resourced identity programmes operate as effectively and with as much benefit as any other corporate resources.

SECTION 9

Benefits

A corporate identity programme will not succeed by itself in making change. A good corporate identity underlines change and helps it to happen.

The benefits which a corporate identity programme can bring must therefore always be seen as part of a package of corporate changes and improvements.

With this proviso the benefits which a change in corporate identity can bring are as follows:

- It allows the process of change to take place more quickly and easily inside an organisation.
- It enables one company to absorb another with the minimum dislocation.
- It enables organisations to tell the people with whom they deal what they stand for, what they are, what they do and how they do it. It enables them to explain how their activities relate to each other.
- It encourages tighter and more coherent messages of all kinds to emerge from the corporation.
- It enables people who deal with the company to understand its corporate goals and objectives.

Because of these advantages, a well organised corporate identity programme also brings with it other advantages:

INTERNAL

- It can improve morale and motivation internally.
- It can reduce staff turnover.
- It can enable better products of more consistent quality to be produced.

- It can enable the company to attract a better calibre of employee than its more anonymous competitors.
- It can enable people from different parts of the organisation to work together more effectively.

FINANCIAL

- It can make for higher recognition in financial circles, and therefore often favourably affects share prices.
- It can allow for acquisitions to be made with less difficulty.
- It can allow organisations to defend themselves more effectively against potential predators.

MARKETING

- It can encourage consumers to look more favourably upon the company and its products and to stay brand loyal.
- It can encourage suppliers to operate regularly and consistently.
- It can allow for more cost-effective expenditure in terms of activities and promotion.
- It can enable the company to establish itself more effectively in new markets.
- It can allow for the more rapid emergence of new activities within a company.

SECTION 10

Examples

REPSOL

Repsol is Spain's largest single company and one of Europe's major oil companies. It comprised virtually the entire public sector activity of the Spanish oil industry.

Within Repsol there are exploration companies, petro-chemical companies, distribution companies and all of the other activities that go to make up a major oil business. Each of these had its own traditions, name and identity.

INH (Instituto Nacional Hydrocarburos), the state holding company for Spain's energy business of which the Repsol companies were a part, recognised both the threat and the opportunity presented by the single European market.

In 1986 it began reviewing its identity. Wolff Olins were appointed and presented a programme in which a monolithic identity using the name Repsol replaced the various company names, and a new visual style was recommended appropriate for Spain in particular, and European markets as a whole.

Repsol's most visible presence in Spain, which will emerge during the first few years of the 1990s, is the network of 1,000 petrol stations which have been designed as the flagship for the new identity.

The Repsol example embraces all of the aspects of a major corporate identity programme, design in communication, product and environment — and it also has major behavioural implications.

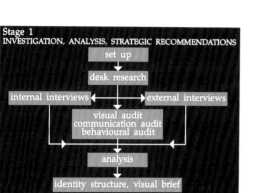

Stage 1
INVESTIGATION, ANALYSIS, STRATEGIC RECOMMENDATIONS

set up

desk research

internal interviews ◄────────► external interviews

visual audit
communication audit
behavioural audit

analysis

identity structure, visual brief

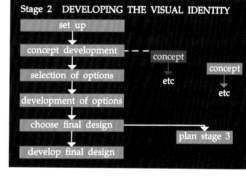

Stage 2   DEVELOPING THE VISUAL IDENTITY

set up

concept development - - -   concept   concept

selection of options   etc   etc

development of options

choose final design ──────────► plan stage 3

develop final design

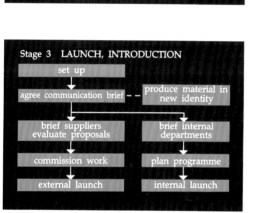

Stage 3   LAUNCH, INTRODUCTION

set up

agree communication brief - -   produce material in
                                 new identity

brief suppliers   brief internal
evaluate proposals   departments

commission work   plan programme

external launch   internal launch

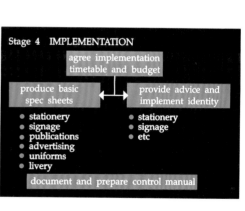

Stage 4   IMPLEMENTATION

agree implementation
timetable and budget

produce basic   provide advice and
spec sheets ◄────────►   implement identity

- stationery   - stationery
- signage   - signage
- publications   - etc
- advertising
- uniforms
- livery

document and prepare control manual

PRUDENTIAL CORPORATION

During the course of the 1990s the various different organisations of which the financial sector is comprised will become more similar and uniform and more directly competitive with each other in terms of the products and services they offer.

Banks, insurance companies, building societies and other organisations are all presenting the same products to the market place, at about the same price, sold in much the same way.

In this situation, each major financial organisation needs to differentiate itself from its competitors as clearly as it can. Many have decided to develop clear and powerful identity programmes.

The Prudential Corporation is one of Britain's largest financial services groups. In addition to its long-standing life assurance activities, the base upon which its fortunes were founded, it is the largest single investor on the London Stock Exchange and one of the biggest and most successful unit trust organisations. It has also become Britain's largest estate agent.

The Prudential Corporation's identity was fragmented; it used different names and different visual symbols in different places. However, it was largely symbolised by the Victorian chief office in Holborn (designed by Alfred Waterhouse), the idea of 'the Mighty Pru', the major City investor, and perhaps above all by 'the Man from the Pru'. None of these images represented the contemporary reality.

Wolff Olins, who were the consultants, recommended replacing the fragmentation with a monolithic structure and creating a new visual style around a modern interpretation of Prudence, a traditional icon of the organisation, after whom it was named.

The Prudential Corporation's identity was fragmented. The organisation projected itself through a variety of images of which the most potent were the Chief Office, designed by Waterhouse (top) and the idea of the 'Man from the Pru' (middle). These have been replaced by a new interpretation of Prudence created by Wolff Olins.

AKZO

Akzo was formed from a series of mergers in 1964. It is Holland's fourth largest company and one of the world's top 20 chemical companies. It operates in 50 countries, 300 locations and employs 70,000 people. It is involved in a range of businesses that includes chemicals, fibres, coatings and products for healthcare. When the company was first formed the intention was to create and sustain a federation of companies, each of which was well-known and regarded in its own field: Sikkens in paint and coatings, Organon in pharmaceuticals, Enka in fibres and so on. The Akzo identity was not emphasised.

However, by the early 1980s it became clear that lack of cohesion was inhibiting the organisation's ability to recruit, to make acquisitions, to co-ordinate research and to develop new products across divisions.

It was decided that a corporate identity programme should be developed that would enable the company to present itself as a major player in chemicals worldwide in the same league as ICI, Hoechst, Bayer Dow, Du Pont and others.

Most chemical companies market the same kind of products at about the same kind of price, in the same sort of way. What primarily distinguishes them is the way in which they do their business.

Akzo is very decentralised and because it delegates so much authority down the line it needs also to focus on the individual and his or her achievements. These attitudes inspired the identity, which was created by Wolff Olins.

The design of the symbol was based on a Greek bas relief originally placed (in about 450 BC) outside a place of education, and used a measuring gauge as well as a symbol.

This bas relief was adapted for the purposes required by a corporate identity programme for a modern global corporation.

Akzo (top) the original symbol, and (bottom) the new Akzo symbol designed by Wolff Olins which replaced it and has been used on a much wider and more comprehensive scale by the organisation.

ICI

ICI is one of the leading UK companies and a major player in the international chemicals business. Since the late 1970s ICI has increasingly moved away from its UK dominated commodity type business and into a series of added value activities some of which it dominates worldwide.

It has, for example, become the largest paint manufacturer in the world. In paints it owns a number of businesses each of which has its own name and reputation and its own market place.

ICI needed to demonstrate its size and strength in markets such as Japan and the US, where it is not so well-known and established, by associating itself clearly with those brands and companies which it had acquired without diluting the strength of ICI. Each ICI activity was given an opportunity through a sliding scale of endorsement of associating itself closely or distantly from the whole organisation.

It also needed to reinforce and emphasise its identity in those markets in which it had already established a high profile. Wolff Olins was appointed to carry out this work.

The major and most significant audience for the ICI identity programme was its own staff.

The existing visual identity was slightly modified, the colour changed and the traditional roundel modulated. New and stricter rules were introduced for application of the identity, and perhaps most importantly, a new system of endorsement was introduced.

This enabled ICI (the group) to derive further strength in some market places where it was not particularly well known by associating itself with the brands and companies which it had acquired and which were well known. These in turn drew strength from ICI's world-class reputation.

Over the years ICI's logotype has been modified from
time to time to keep it up to date. The major purpose
of the identity programme created by Wolff Olins was
to manage ICI's visual imagery in a more
co-ordinated fashion so that its different brands and
companies retain an appropriate degree of independence
while clearly being seen as part of a corporate whole.

CONCLUSION

The future for corporate identity

The corporate identity business is growing at about 25% to 30% per year incrementally. The figures vary a bit by country and by industry type, but the trend is clear. Why?

The main reasons are the following, not necessarily in order of importance:

First; in one industry after another the bad companies go to the wall and the better companies all make products whose characteristics are similar. It is virtually impossible to detect quality differences between the products of major financial service companies, or petrol retailers or the various chemical companies for instance.

This means that companies and their brands have increasingly to compete with each other on emotional rather than rational grounds. The company with the strongest, most consistent, most attractive, best implemented and manifested reputation/identity will emerge on top in this race. Look at how the Prudential has emerged in the world of financial services since it introduced a new identity.

Second; organisations are spinning into and away from each other at ever increasing speeds. New forms of company are emerging like Airbus with French, German, British, Spanish and Dutch participants. Strategic alliances are being formed like Alsthom GEC which is a Franco-British association between subsidiaries of two major companies which remain in competition in other fields. Mergers take place within Europe, like ABB from Sweden and Switzerland and between European and US companies like Beecham and Smith Kline.

These new companies cannot be formed without a new identity. The new name and the symbolism are put in place to create new loyalties, replace old ones, help support new working practices make the outside world aware of the new force — and above all to get the internal team all thinking the same way and acting as though they are on the same side.

Third; fewer babies are being born in well-off countries. This means in the longer term that the pool of potential recruits for business will be reduced and that companies will have to fight harder to get good people. Inevitably then, companies are learning to market themselves not only to consumers, but also to potential employees. Those companies with powerful, consistent attractive identities have a great advantage.

Fourth; perhaps the single most important audience for the company will be its own employees. Having recruited them, probably at considerable trouble and expense, the corporation will have to keep them fulfilled. In a world in which change and reorganisation is a continuing factor in working life, companies are using their identities to hold the workforce together.

Fifth; the indications are that the corporation is becoming increasingly involved with society. Sponsorship is a sign of this. Sponsorship in consumer affairs, in health, education, the environment and other areas is becoming the norm. Companies increasingly are judged in some respects and by some communities as much for their attitudes towards their social responsibilities as for profitability. The company with the strong identity and acceptable social behaviour is becoming popular and noticeable.

All this means that companies will move from dealing with one single major target audience — the consumer, to forming a multiplicity of relationships with a number of significant target audiences — consumers, recruits, host communities and so on.

This in turn means that identity will be at the heart of everything that the corporation does, says, makes, sells, because the corporation's identity will be the major resource which it will use to differentiate itself from its competitors to all of the complex audiences with which it deals.

All this indicates that over time no major organisation will be without its corporate identity, which will enable it to make its strategy and culture visible.

BIBLIOGRAPHY

Here are a few books which a general reader on the subject may find both interesting and useful.

The books chosen deal not only with design, but also with business, history and art. All these are proper subjects for the study of identity.

Banham, R. *Theory and Design in the First Machine Age*, Architectural Press, 1960

Bernstein, David. *Company Image and Reality*, Architectural Press: Holt, Rinehart & Winston, 1984

Betjeman, J. *London's Historic Railway Stations*, John Murray, 1972

Bowers, Michael. *Railway Styles in Building*, Almark, 1975

Caplan, Ralph. *By Design*, St Martins Press, 1982

Handy, C. *Understanding Organisations*, Penguin, 1986

Heller, Robert. *The New Naked Manager*, Hodder & Stoughton, rev ed, 1985

Hobsbawm, E. and Ranger, T. *The Invention of Tradition*, Cambridge University Press, 1983

Hudson, L. *Contrary Imaginations*, Penguin, 1968

Koestler, P. *The Act of Creation*, Hutchinson, 1976

Kuhn, T. S. *The Structure of the Scientific Revolution*, University of Chicago, 1970

Levitt, T. *The Marketing Imagination*, The Free Press, 1983

Lorenz, C. *Design Dimensions*, Basil Blackwell, 1986

Olins, W. *Corporate Identity*, Thames & Hudson, 1989

Papanek, V. *Design for the Real World*, Thames & Hudson, 2nd ed, 1985

Pevsner, N. *Pioneers of Modern Design*, Penguin, 2nd ed, 1960

Pilditch, J. *Communication by Design*, McGraw, 1970
  Talk About Design, Barrie & Jenkins, 1976

Porter, Michael E. *Competitive Advantage*, Collier Macmillan, 1985

Rolt, L. T. C. *Isambard Kingdom Brunel*, Penguin, 1985

Trevor-Roper, H. *Princes and Artists: Patronage and Ideology of four Habsburg Courts 1577–1633*, Thames & Hudson, 1976

Simon, Herbert A. *The Sciences of the Artificial*, MIT Press, 1981

Sloan, A. *My Years with General Motors*, Doubleday & Co, New York, 1984

Storr, Antony. *The Dynamics of Creation*, Penguin, 1976

Whitfield, P. R. *Creativity in Industry*, Penguin, 1975

Wiener, M. *English Culture and the Decline of the Industrial Spirit 1850–1980*, Cambridge University Press, 1982

APPENDIX A

These are the basic elements that make up the visual system of a corporate identity:

- the name
- subsidiary names (if appropriate)
- symbol
- major typeface
- subsidiary typefaces (if appropriate)
- colours

APPENDIX B

This is a standard checklist of items over which the visual elements are usually applied. Experience indicates that it is appropriate for most companies, but it may need modifying in particular cases.

PRODUCTS AND SERVICES

Products

- product design
- product identification
- rating plates
- operating instructions
- calibration instructions

Packaging

- inners
- outer cartons
- labelling
- delivery instructions
- installation instructions

ENVIRONMENTS

Interiors/exteriors

- buildings
- reception areas
- sales areas

- offices
- factories
- shops
- showrooms

Signs

- main identification
- general sign system internal/external

EXHIBITIONS

Clothing

- badges
- safety hats
- overalls
- lab coats
- smocks

COMMUNICATION MATERIALS

Stationery

- letterheads
- continuation sheets
- memos
- compliment slips
- visiting cards
- envelopes
- postal labels

Forms

- accounting
- purchasing
- sales
- production
- personnel

Publications

- corporate
- personnel/training
- industry packages
- product

Vehicles

- road transport
- factory transport

Advertising

- corporate
- recruitment
- product/services

Promotions/giveaways

- flags
- stickers
- ties
- promotional and point-of-sale material

APPENDIX C

DESIGN ADVISORY SERVICES

The Chartered Society of Designers (CSD)

29 Bedford Square

London WC1B 3EG

01-631 1510

The Design Council

28 Haymarket

London SW1Y 4SU

01-839 8000

Design Management Institute

364 Brookline Avenue

Boston Mass 02215

(617) 236 4165

Incorporated Society of British Advertisers (ISBA)

44 Hertford Street

London W1Y 8AE

01-499 7502

Institute of Public Relations (IPR)

1 St Johns Square

London EC1M 4DH

01-253 5151